# FIRST TECHNOLOGY
# Toys

Author: **John Williams**
Photography: **Zul Mukhida**

Dear Santa,
This year I've been good,
and so I wondered if you would
please bring me toys instead of socks.
(I really have got lots and lots!)

Thank you. Hope you get this letter,

Lots of love from

Henrietta

**W**
HODDER
*Wayland*

an imprint of Hodder Children's Books

# FIRST TECHNOLOGY

## Titles in this series

Machines

Tools

Wheels and Cogs

Energy

Toys

Packaging

Series editor: Kathryn Smith
Designer: Loraine Hayes

First published in Great Britain in 1993
by Wayland (Publishers) Ltd
Reprinted in 2001 by Hodder Wayland,
an imprint of Hodder Children's Books

**British Library Cataloguing in Publication Data**

Williams, John
Toys – (First Technology Series)
I. Title II. Series
688.7

ISBN 0 7502 3406 7

Typeset by DJS Fotoset Ltd, Burgess Hill, Sussex.
Printed and bound in Hong Kong

**Acknowledgements**
The publishers would like to thank Canterbury Bears and all their
staff for their kind help and co-operation. All the photographs in this
book were taken by Zul Mukhida, except for the following:
John Caldwell 6-11, 19, 20; Chapel Studios 18 (John Heinrich);
GGS 6-7.

WARNING: Toys which are made badly can be dangerous. Make
sure that children play with toys which have been rigourously tested
and meet the appropriate safety standards.

Words printed in **bold**
appear in the glossary on
page 31.

Toys are made in all shapes, sizes and colours.
They are made for children of all ages.
Do you have any toys like these at home?

Hayley and Daniel are playing with their favourite board game.

Do you have a favourite toy or game?

Children have always played with toys.
These toys were made about 100 years ago.
Are they like the toys you play with?

6

These toys are even older.
The jigsaw was made
over 200 years ago.

These metal cutters are used to cut pieces of cloth.
The pieces are used to make a toy.
Can you guess what the toy is?

The pieces of cloth are stitched together to make a head, a body, arms and legs.

Special **joints** are put inside the arms and legs.

A machine blows **stuffing** into the toy.

9

All the holes are sewn up by hand.

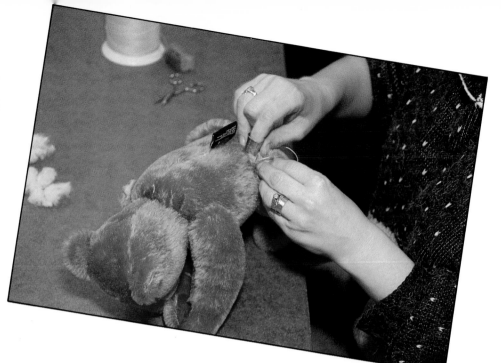

Fur is shaved off the **face**.

10

The nose is carefully sewn in place.

The teddy bear is finished!

11

Toys work in
different ways.
Hayley pushes
these cars
to make
them move.

This toy caterpillar needs to be pulled along to make it move.

What do you have to do to make this scooter move?

This toy train works by clockwork. Melissa winds it up with a key. When she takes the key out the wheels of the train turn round.

14

This remote-control car needs **electricity** to make it work.

The car has **batteries** inside. The batteries make electricity.
Do you know how Hayley makes the car stop, start and turn round?

This electronic game needs
electricity to work too.
Do you like playing with
electronic games?

Hayley pushes down with her hands on this top, to make it spin round. The top spins round very quickly.

These toys are puppets. You can make them move and dance by pulling on their strings.
Where are the people who make the puppets work?

18

This is a computer game. Computer games are a modern toy. There were no computer games thirty years ago.

19

You could build a model like this. It has **levers** and **pulley wheels** to make it work.

Daniel is looking through a kaleidoscope. When light shines through, Daniel can see pretty patterns.

Joseph is holding a kite. What does the kite need to make it fly?

21

This jigsaw puzzle is nearly finished. Can you see how the pieces fit together?

You need to think carefully when you play with a puzzle toy.

These old toys are made from **materials** that are not used for making toys anymore.

**Tin** train

**China** doll

**Lead** soldiers

23

These three modern toys are made of **plastic**. Plastic can be made into any shape we like.

24

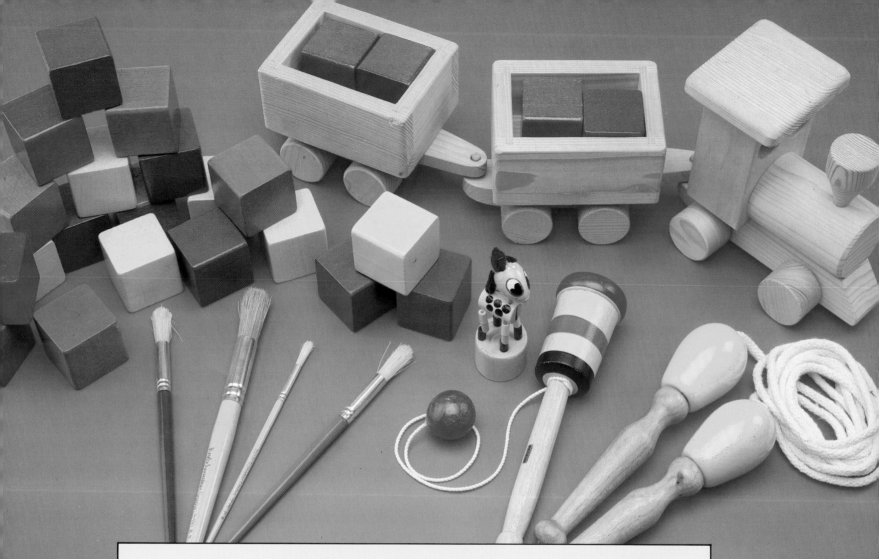

Not all modern toys are made of plastic. These new toys are all made of the same material. Do you know what it is?

You can make your own toys out of all sorts of different materials. How many different kinds of materials can you see in this picture?

Melissa is making a toy car. Can you see what she is using to make it?

# Making a jumping machine

1. Cut the rubber band in one place.

2. Stick the rubber band to each side of the cotton reel with sticky tape.

3. Slide the cotton reel over the wooden dowel, and fix the middle of the rubber band to the top of the dowel with more tape.

4. Put the end of the dowel on a table and pull the cotton reel down. Stand clear and let go!

# NOTES FOR TEACHERS AND PARENTS

Play is a vital part of a child's development, and toys are an essential part of this process. They provide both a stimulus for the imagination, and a focus for the child's pretend world.

Toys can also introduce children to other aspects of the wider world. The materials from which toys are made, and their design and testing, are all parts of manufacturing processes.

How a toy works, whether by electricity, steam, sound or a rubber band, can introduce children to the concept of energy. Toys that need to be pushed or pulled can introduce children to the concept of forces.

Making their own toys will help children to develop greater manual dexterity and will allow them to test their own observational skills. They will also gain firsthand experience of simple scientific and technological processes.

## Making the Jumping Machine

This simple machine obtains its energy from the stretched rubber band. It transforms the potential (or waiting energy) of the stretched rubber band into the kinetic (or moving energy) of the jumping toy. These two forms of energy combine to produce mechanical energy. Older children can use this toy as a push-pull force measurer. For this purpose a slightly longer piece of dowel should be used.

# GLOSSARY

**Batteries** Special objects which make electricity.

**China** A very fine sort of clay which breaks quite easily.

**Electricity** A kind of energy that makes things work.

**Joints** Special pieces used in toy-making. They allow the arms, legs and heads of the toys to move and bend.

**Lead** A kind of metal. It can be poisonous.

**Levers** Bars of metal, plastic or wood, which are used to help lift things.

**Material** What something is made from. Metal, plastic, cloth, wood, china, tin, lead and paper are all kinds of materials.

**Plastic** A special kind of material which can be made into any shape we like.

**Pulley wheel** A wheel with a groove round it. A rope or chain fits in the groove. Pulley wheels are used to help lift things.

**Stuffing** Special material used to fill soft toys.

**Tin** A kind of metal.

# INDEX